THE CHRISTMAS STORY

ILLUSTRATED BY STEPHANIE RYDER

Brimax . Newmarket . England

Long ago, in a town called Nazareth, there lived a young woman named Mary. One day a great light appeared and the angel Gabriel stood before her. "Do not be afraid," said the angel. "I bring you joyful news. God has chosen you to be the mother of his son. You will have a baby and you must call him Jesus."

In the same town there lived a carpenter named Joseph. Joseph loved Mary very much. He was going to marry her. The angel came to visit Joseph and told him that Mary was going to have God's son. Later Joseph came to see Mary and told her what the angel had said.

One day a message came from the governor of the land. All of the people had to go back to the place where they had been born so they could be counted. Joseph was worried. He and Mary would have to go to Bethlehem. This was a long way away and Mary was almost ready to have her baby.

They set off early the next morning. Joseph led the way. Mary rode on a donkey. The road was long and hard. They didn't reach Bethlehem until the evening. The town was full of people. Joseph tried everywhere to find a place to stay, but all the rooms were taken. Mary was so tired she could hardly stay awake.

At last an innkeeper said, "All my rooms are full, but you can use my stable. It is clean and warm in there."
Joseph thanked him and they went inside. All around them cows and donkeys lay peacefully asleep. The hay was soft and smelled sweet. Mary and Joseph lay down and rested.

In the night, Mary gave birth to her baby. It was a boy as the angel had said. They named him Jesus.

Mary wrapped him in a blanket and laid him in a manger, where it was soft and warm.

Mary and Joseph watched over Jesus lovingly. They knew he was a very special baby.

Out on the hillside above the town, some shepherds were looking after their sheep. Suddenly the sky was filled with light and an angel appeared. The shepherds fell to the ground in fear.

But the angel said, "Do not be afraid. I bring you good news. Today a child is born. He is the son of God. You will find him in Bethlehem, lying in a manger."

The shepherds gazed in wonder as the sky was filled with angels singing.

"We must go and find this child," said one. "We can take one of our newborn lambs as a gift."

They went to Bethlehem and found Jesus in the stable with Mary and Joseph. They fell to their knees and offered their gift.

Far away in an eastern land lived some wise men. One night they saw a bright new star in the sky. They wanted to know what it meant. They looked in their books for the answer. "It means that a new king has been born," they said. "We must go and look for him so that we can worship him. The star will guide us."

The wise men set off on their journey. The star shone brightly in front of them by day and by night. They came to the palace of King Herod who said to them, "You must find the new king then tell me where he is." King Herod was not very pleased.

The wise men followed the star for many miles. It stopped right over the stable where Jesus lay. "We are looking for the newborn king," they said. "A bright star has guided us from far away." Joseph led them into the stable. They knelt before Jesus and offered him some very special gifts of gold, frankincense and myrrh.

The next day, the wise men set out for King Herod's palace. They stopped to rest and while they were asleep an angel came to them in a dream. "Do not go back to Herod," the angel warned. "He does not want Jesus to be King." The wise men decided to go home a different way.

Mary and Joseph were very happy and proud. They knew their baby was really the son of God. They knew he was very special and that he would have important work to do when he grew up. They also knew that Jesus would be loved throughout the world and that people would remember his birth as a time of happiness and peace.

Say these words again.

carpenter	star
message	palace
donkey	special
stable	dream
blanket	happiness
sheep	bright
gift	worship